There once was an opossum named Meatball who lived in a tree. He was called Meatball because that was his favorite thing to eat and because after he ate all the meatballs he wanted, he usually rolled around like one too.

One day Meatball saw a piece of paper blowing down the street. It stopped long enough for him to see it. There was a picture of a man wearing a big top hat, a black tux, and white gloves with people on their feet cheering for him. There was a sign above him that said Marvin the Magnificent. Meatball decided he wanted to be like that too, so he went home, packed his things, and started off towards the brightest lights he could find.

When he arrived at the place with the bright lights, he found out it was a park! With other animals! There were no people around, so Meatball quietly slipped over the fence and began walking around, wanting to visit with the other animals.

The first place he visited was a deep blue pool. Meatball put his toe in the water and it was freezing! Suddenly, a giant whale came bursting out of the water right in front of him, then came crashing down with a mighty **SPLASH**. The wave flew up and drenched poor Meatball. "I'm sorry about that," the whale said to Meatball, "I didn't mean to scare you, or to splash you either."

"It's okay," Meatball said, "I wasn't too scared anyways. What's your name?"

"My name's Wendell, what's yours?"

"My name is Meatball the Magnificent! Or, at least it will be when I become famous." Meatball said proudly.

"Oh you want to be a performer in a show? We have a show here every day and people come from all around just to see us! They love to see me leap high in the air and come crashing down! Then, I swim around my pool and splash people, just for fun!"

That didn't sound like a lot of fun to Meatball, but he didn't want to be impolite. "Why don't you show me?" Meatball asked. Wendell nodded. First, he swam around his pool, dove really deep, and then came flying up before crashing down with a mighty splash! Meatball didn't get wet this time, until Wendell flipped over and flicked water at him with his tail. That did get him wet.

"Thanks for showing me Wendell, but I don't think this show is for me. I'm not a good swimmer." Meatball said.
"That's okay, there are other shows around here. I'm sure you can fit in somewhere."

Meatball walked off and soon found himself walking through a big dark cave. As he walked he heard a strange, scary sound. "Hello? Is anyone there?" **Grrrr** "My name's Meatball the Magnificent and I'm looking to join a show." **Grrrr** Suddenly a big lion came running out of the cave, jumped on top of a big rock and let out a mighty roar. Meatball was so scared that he fainted.

"Are you okay?" the lion asked him when he woke up.
"I'm okay, you just scared me a little." Meatball answered.
"Oh, I'm sorry." The lion said, "My name is Leona. Your name is Meatball the Magnificent right?" Meatball nodded. "I've never heard of you, but if you want to join my show, you have to be loud! That's what I do. I come out, stand on this rock, and roar as loud as I can. People love to hear me roar. Do you roar?" Meatball had never tried to roar, but he thought he could.

He took a deep breath and roared as loud as he could. All that came out was a hiss. "I don't want to be rude," Leona said, "but I don't think that's loud enough. Keep practicing though, and maybe you could come join the show one day." Meatball thanked Leona for her advice and left.

Very quickly.

He started climbing up and soon found himself face to face with a very strange looking animal. It had hair like his, and a long curly tail like his, but instead of a long pointed nose and claws on its hands, it had a very flat face and fingers, like a person. "Hello," the animal said, "my names Myron, and I'm a monkey. What's your name?"

"I am Meatball the Magnificent! Do you have a show here?" Meatball asked.

"You bet! People come from all around just to watch my family and I play in the trees. We climb up and down, swing from branch to branch, and jump to the ground from way up high." This sounded like something Meatball could do.

"Well I can climb trees," Meatball said, "and I can hang from the branches, but I don't jump or swing."

"Oh that's easy, you should try it." Myron said. So Meatball climbed out onto the highest limb he could reach. Then he wrapped his tail around the limb and lowered himself down.

"That's good," Myron said, "now just swing and jump off!"

Meatball suddenly became very scared. He tried to swing, but his body and tail wouldn't move.

"I don't think I can do this." Meatball said. "I've never climbed up this high before, and I can't make myself swing like you."

"That's okay, maybe some other time." Myron said.

Meatball left the strange tree. He didn't want to go home yet, but the sun was coming up so he climbed a nearby normal tree and fell asleep. He was woken up by a loud shout and lots of shaking.

He looked down and saw two men in brown clothes looking up at him. He didn't know who they were, but maybe they were here to see his show! He quickly remembered everything he had learned the night before.

First, he leaped high in the air like Wendell taught him...

Then he tried to flick water on them from a fountain but they didn't like that very much.

Next, he tried to roar like Leona taught him, but he only hissed again.

...but when he swung out, his tail slipped and he started falling.

Just before he hit ground, one of the men caught him. They put him in a large cage that was in the back of their truck...

and drove him all the way back to the park where he lived.

They let him out of the cage and he quickly ran back home.

The next day Meatball's friend Sally came over to visit.

"We missed you last night Meatball. Where were you?"

Meatball told her his story from the strange park and showed her everything he learned. When he was finished, Sally was amazed.

"Wow Meatball that was an amazing story and a great show!" Sally went and told all the other animals in the park about it and they all came back the next night.

Made in the USA
Monee, IL
27 November 2023

46840358R00019